Praise

Abandoned Accounts

———————————— ◆ ————————————

"Rather than leave behind what so often fades in memory, the poems in Roy Christopher's *Abandoned Accounts* hold onto each hypercolor detail even as 'giant, plate-glass plans' are made. But the real joy comes from the seemingly random and temporary connections described with sensuous turns of phrase. To borrow a line from 'Body Language', Christopher 'betrays [our] best effort / to remain innocent, quiet, and disengaged.'"

— **Rebecca Guess Cantor**, author, *The Other Half*

"Roy Christopher's *Abandoned Accounts* is an easy conversation in a breezy beer garden with an old friend you haven't seen for years. Talk of music, memories, stolen moments, and philosophical musings share time with stories about life lived in cities across the country. The style is laidback, wandering, and effortless, just like any good conversation should be. Pull up a chair and shoot the shit, you'll be glad you did."

— **Scott Wozniak**, author , *Shooting Gallery Vultures*

"My favorite book of poetry since Lana Del Rey's."

— **Peter Relic**, author, *Ping Pong on the Periodic Table*

"When I read a poem, I am, finally, reading abandonment. Some writers abandon prematurely. Some abandon at the very limits of their gifts. Some abandon and they are ethereal and heavenly abandonments. Perfect abandonments. Those are abandonments I aspire to."
— Carmen Giménez Smith

"Poets don't finish poems, they abandon them."
— Paul Valéry

"The most dramatic finding from the survey was that 66.0% of surveyed blogs had not been updated in two months, representing 2.72 million blogs that have been either permanently or temporarily abandoned."
— Perseus Development Survey, 2003

FIRST CUT

Abandoned
Accounts

Poems 2020-2021

by

Roy Christopher

Close To The Bone Publishing

Contents

◆

Peripatetic

Glimpses

Episodes in Erewhon

Strays

About the Author

◆

Roy Christopher is an aging BMX and skateboarding zine kid. That's where he learned to turn events and interviews into pages with staples. He has since written about music, media, and culture for everything from self-published zines and personal blogs to national magazines and academic journals. He holds a Ph.D. in Communication Studies from the University of Texas at Austin. This is his first collection of poetry.

Keep up with him at www.roychristopher.com

.

Peripatetic

Baldwin Park, Savannah

My neighbor Tony told me to get a haircut.
I was riding my bike on Hamilton Ct.
He was wearing a "double-0 Corndog" t-shirt.
Sitting in his front yard, double-cup drinking,
Playing 2 Chainz on his Beats Pill.

On 44th between Chatham Crescent and Waters,
Halfway between the circle of Theus Park
And the Bananas at Daffin, I found a rabbit:
A double-Dutch, double-stuffed
Oreo Rabbit, with the ears and all.

I asked around and everyone said
It belonged to the neighbors, and
Just roams around.
"Surprised it's still alive,"
One lady said, unconcerned.

The last guy I asked
Acted as annoyed as the rest:
"Yeah, just roams around," he said.
"Got another one," he added,
"Goes with it."

My First Time

My first time downtown
We were killing time in between things
There were elves in green outside on the corner

I lost Nick upstairs when they came in
One gave me a flyer for an art show down the street
She said I should come

I found Nick after they left
And showed him the flyer
He insisted we go to the installation

The show was a furry, fun tour
Of a stuffed-animal forest scene
Hollow trees and knotty murals on the walls

After the show I filled out a comment card
Told the lady in green that it was great
But that she was the best part

She emailed me later that week
And made my new coworkers jealous
I didn't even live in Portland yet

After I moved there, she would come over
With skateboard videos and snacks
Wearing jeans with a hole in the thigh

We were never really together
But one night we made out in the rain
My first time and then never again

Phil Collins

I woke up with a Peter Gabriel song in my head
"I Don't Remember"
I put it on as I was making coffee

I let the record keep going
As I got ready to go to the grocery store
"Games Without Frontiers" was on

While browsing the bulk snacks
A guy walked by
Singing "Games Without Frontiers"

He looked like Richard Simmons
If Richard Simmons were homeless
Pink tank-top, pink running shorts, dirty curly hair

He said he had the song stuck in his head
"Phil Collins, right?" he asked
"Right," I said

Honey Dew Melon

I went to summer school between 11th and 12th grade
So I could have a study hall my senior year

My free period was in Mr. Kelly's English class
I sat in the back by the windows

One day a new girl sat in the row next to me
She wrote the first note

"What's with all the question marks?"
My answer was dumb, but she was undeterred

Fifteen years later, I went to a conference in Salt Lake City
Where she had moved some time before

We fed each other popcorn and ignored a movie
Limbs woven together in her giant beanbag chair

"What's with all the questions?"
Her answer was stern, but I was undeterred

After points and counterpoints, exaltations and explanations
We moved to another room

Her hair was like handles, her polka-dot skirt like a curtain
Over that tender window

In the kitchen,
There was a ripe, round honey dew melon

A few days later I was back at school
And I never took another break

In Chicago

In Chicago,
I always lived in half-basements
Garden Apartments, they call them there

Never fully underground
But always potentially buried
By the weight of the stories overhead

One night
I heard my upstairs neighbor crying
Through the floor

I would've gone up
To check on her
But I was already crying myself

Harness

Now we know there's no harness wrapped around our waist,
It's only a hand clasping our arm.

New To You

A trail hot
With footfalls
And information

The prints condense
In headlines, deadlines, and hit lists
A path without math

Brain and bones aching
From walking through words
Like worlds

I misread "picnic" as "panic"
And "enjoyed" as "annoyed"
My stamina waning

Alarm replaced regularly
Outrage runs down like batteries
Or out like fossil fuels

Don't you just miss
When more things were new
To you

The Mysteries Of Spring Break

Sitting in a creaky swing
On the beach in Florida
Watching the clouds and waves
When a young man approached.

He sat down and asked me
To choose 3 animals:
"One from on land, one aquatic,
And one of the air."

I thought for a second and said,
"On land, a rabbit,
In water, a whale,
And in the air, a cardinal."

He contemplated my answers
Longer than I liked
Before he got up to leave
Without prognosis or prophecy.

I'm not sure if I hit the jackpot
On some psychotic lottery
Or if he was just high
On the mysteries of spring break.

Backlit

Backlit by burning bridges
Our silhouettes flickering on the floor
We sat on the suitcases
Of a dead love, packed and fleeing

Yours was a landscape
I wanted to explore on hands and knees
Then mow down and set on fire
Like scattered leaves and leveled trees

Our dear friend seemed to see something else
When she said, "Who knew we were
Already who we were going to be?"
So, we did it again, against that shared history

With a violence we had never visited
We tried at last to make it last
Knowing it was already over
Yet somehow still aching to make it stay

After giving it an ending
Finally, we gave it up
Letting it burn with the rest
Close as ghosts until the last

Ready For Adventure

There's a story in there.
It's a story about your mouth.
It's a story about your lips.
About the contours of your smile.
About the shape of your face
       when you laugh,
       when you sigh,
       when you moan,
       when you cry out.

It's a story about your head.
It's a story about your eyes.
About the universes bound up in them.
About the way they expand,
       the way they swirl,
       the way they blink,
       the way they squeeze
       shut against the feeling.

It's a story about your body.
It's a story about its curves.
About the bend of your being.
About the places unseen,
       the unexplored,
       the places untouched
       that need attention.

It's a story about your spirit.
It's a story about your way.
About your absence.
About your influence
> from a distance
> from so far,
> from the outside.

It's a story about you sitting
At the end of the bed,
Your slight shoulders
Atop a torso that pools
Into hips and thighs
Like you were poured there
> then paused,
> poised...
> Ready for adventure.

This Morning World

Trees sway in mid-conversation,
Subtly gesticulating to each other.

I always say Good Morning
To the squirrels gathering their breakfast.

Beer bottles and empty chip bags
Litter the sites of parties the night before.

Rabbits are good at a lot of things,
but cleaning up after themselves is not one of them.

Walking dogs always say Hi even if their owners don't,
Their leashes taut against tight grips.

Motorcycles sleep late,
Tucked tight under their covers.

Trains groan against the cold,
Grumbling toward the city's center.

Cars wait in neat rows along the streets as others cough at
intersections,
Their hot breath visible beyond their bumpers.

Leaves scurry indiscriminately.
One more early morning left this semester.

Then this morning world
Will have to live without me.

Third New Tape

The first time I drove
Across the whole United States
I got 3 new cassettes for the trip
I kept them wrapped in plastic until I left

Talking Songs for Walking
By Lungfish was one
"We live with collision," said Daniel Higgs
"We strap ourselves in"

Another was *Boces* by Mercury Rev
Their last record with David Baker
"My primitive words match my primitive heart"
He sang before he left

Between those two
Various other cassettes
And the backlog of unlabeled mixes
I don't remember what the third new tape was

Pale Blue Eyes

I woke up on the couch
At the 18th Street House
There was no sign of life
Save the sound of "Pale Blue Eyes"

I only had a sleeping spot
Because someone else got popped
The night before in The City
Trespassing and tagging graffiti

Smelling old beer and stale perfume
I thought of you as my moon
As the sun of afternoon
Stripped and striped the room

San Diego

The terminal juvenilia of San Diego
Days without end, nonstop sunshine
Carrying a skateboard more than riding it
But being afraid to leave it at home

Sitting outside at Lestat's
We made giant, plate-glass plans
While a kid tried to steal my bike
Two feet from our entwined fingers

I used to ride that S&M Holmes
Seven and a half miles to work
Through sidewalks, train tracks, and one-way streets
But I usually got a ride back to Normal Heights

One day I read Kahlil Gibran aloud
On the round grassy moguls by the Ralph's
Where I later shoplifted for the third time that week
A big bottle of yellow mustard

Tell Me Twice

"'No one's going to stop you', I said to myself,"
I was telling my friend.
"I said it with the dumb joy of oblivion
I often felt in those days."

It was true. No one ever stopped me.
Now that dumb joy is gone with the drink.
Now it's just a dull shame attached to hazy,
Half-remembered scenes like that one.

The memory hung hard like so many mornings after.
In the weeks that followed, I'd really only slid
From day drunk to dry drunk,
And I realized how far metaphors can fall.

I grabbed his shoulder thoughtfully
As I arrived at the statement,
"A lot of things can be a lot of things."
"You don't have to tell me twice," he said.

Infinite Jest

We hurried home from the bar
Fueled by fear, alcohol,
And the excitement of escape
Into the possibilities of each other

Her keys were like stray puzzle pieces,
And in her room, she tackled me,
Pinned me, and kissed me
In front of her half-empty bookshelf

She had three books by Cornel West
Next to David Foster Wallace's *Infinite Jest*
Said she'd never read it, but
Had "started it several times"

Spoiler

She said she didn't like the idea
Of an allergy medication
That needed to "build up" in her body
To be effective

We'd just done several sloppy lines
Off of a spoiler bolted to
The back of a red Sentra
Parked crooked on East 6th

Halfway through a long weekend
We were walking west
As it started to rain
I don't remember how we made it home

The day my bed and my refrigerator are in separate rooms
I will miss the sound of the compressor cycling on
Like a dream monitor
Carrying me safely to the next morning

Loud Yet Hushed

It sounded like something
In the clutches of something else
In the clutches of itself

It felt long yet rushed
Loud yet hushed
Pulled taut against itself

Vulnerable yet bulletproof
I could feel it
With every cell of my self

A con and a contradiction
Like getting what you want
In spite of yourself

The One That Got Away

I didn't apply, I was recruited
I didn't realize until I did
That I was wrong
About the one that got away

So far and so unwilling
To meet anywhere near the middle
I'm standing still here, and
You're going the other way

I know you don't like
What you bring out in me
Which is a convenient way
Of blaming you for my own behavior

I might not be able to take a hint
But I'm pretty perceptive, and I know
What a relief it would be
To never hear from me again

Reckless

These days are thankless, ruthless, and reckless.
They hold no truck with your wishes or your whims.
A week of them will crush you and brush you aside.

You can be clean, pure, good intentioned.
You can be mean, conniving, vindictive.
It matters not to the day, to the night, to the time in which you live.

You can work and scheme and hope and anticipate.
Where will you be when it all goes dark?
None of it will matter when the lights flicker out and the sun sets at
last.

Exhausted Explorers

The grass has grown up around us
Blade by blade by blade
Like weeds or leads or leaves on trees
Cutting us low

We fight to translate this light
Filtered through clouds
And the fog of talk
A choked sense of sense

With the luck of thieves
And the arrogance of innocents
We are exhausted explorers
Of a world spent spinning

Scattered Applause

Found Footage,
Wild lines, and bad looping
Lips out of sync with their voices
[Reading the closed captions]

Motion capture,
Green screens, and deep fakes
No telling who or what we're really watching
[Voice-over, overhead, overheard]

Side-eyed aside,
Winking glance, and a tongue askew
It might mean that or its opposite
(Every punchline explained in parentheticals)

Stiff performances,
A bad script, and sloppy shooting
This thing is going nowhere
(The director seems drunk)

An expected plot twist,
An intermission, and three endings
Not sure if it's even over
[Scattered applause]

Virga

Nothing but bad news
On days like these
We're not paying dues
We're just paying fees

When everybody robs
It's less help than hurt
They're not creating jobs
They're just creating work

A longing, a pining
An unrequited sin
Like sun you see shining
But can't feel on your skin

Always dipping below a deficit
Some birds weren't meant to fly
Some of us trying to get away with it
Others just trying to get by

They always have an answer
Unless there are actually questions
I guess this brave cancer
Is finally coming to kill us

A search ongoing
Unfulfilling within
Like wind you see blowing
But can't feel on your skin

They claim they're planting seeds
We swallow pills for pain in the head
They're really burying the leads
While we bury our dead

A door you can't enter
Not even a little
You're not in the center
But you're stuck in the middle

A question still stalling
To quiet the din
Like rain you see falling
But can't feel on your skin

Glimpses

Backstage At SXSW

Backstage at SXSW is a circus and a zoo
I interrupted a blunt cypher
That included Bam Margera
And Erika Badu

I met Bill Murray
Watching GZA perform
I shook his hand
And nodded at the stage

After the show we followed them –
Bill Murray, GZA, Ninth Prince, and others –
Across the street to Shangri-La
Where Bill Murray tended bar

No matter what you ordered
You got a shot of tequila
Apparently, he'd done this before
"Bill's a fool," Ninth Prince told me

Slayer Hat

In 1996
I interviewed Jeff Hanneman
For a piece on Slayer

The story landed in *Ride BMX Magazine*
And the band were so stoked
Their publicist said they were going
To send me something

My friends all speculated:
Something bloody? Something dead?
Something too scary to imagine?
In the end, it was only a hat

I finally saw Slayer play live in 2009
Then Hanneman passed in 2013
I still have the hat though

Not Ready

Korn's first record broke in 1995
While on tour with KMFDM
I managed to catch them
At the Moore Theatre in Seattle

God Lives Underwater opened the show
By the third song, the lead singer
Replaced all the lyrics with expletives
Because everyone was yelling for Korn

During the opening chords of "Blind"
A blonde girl dove off the balcony backwards
Just as Jonathan Davis growled
"Are you rrrrrready?"

As she disappeared over the rail
And into the twist of limbs below
I decided that no,
I was not ready

Thankfully the people on the floor were
And caught her in a net of arms and hands
Most of us left before KMFDM
The real show was over

Yum Yeto

I used to work in the center
Of an industry without a winter
We commandeered some office space at Tum Yeto
While the team manager was out on tour

I shared his desk with another
All makeshift and shift-lock
We were building an e-commerce website
Or pretending to in the meantime

Ed Templeton wandered in once
And introduced himself during lunch
I said I know who you are
But no one else is around

Otis Barthoulameu checked his messages on my phone
Exene Cervenka had called him twice
He casually flipped through my CDs
Voivod, *Nothingface*: "You don't see that very often"

Ethan Fowler friended me on Friendster
Then at the Ken Club, I saw Neil Blender
Kristian Svitak, Corey Duffel, and Lance Conklin
Another time I had coffee with Duane Pitre

I remember the first time they paged Josh Beagle
Years later we would relearn feebles-to-fakies
On the in-house, warehouse mini-ramp
I fell and broke an ink pen in my Dickies pocket

Kim Gordon

Unseasonably sunny Chicago day
All the tables were outside
I was having a beer on the patio
At Logan Bar & Grill

I saw Kim Gordon
Strolling down California Avenue
In crumpled jeans
And a light jacket

Her father was the sociologist
Who named the high-school cliques
You know, jocks and geeks and soshes
I wonder where she sat at lunch

Something in her eyes that day
Said please don't recognize me
So, against all I wanted to say
I just looked and looked away

The wild goddess
Of art and independence
I tweeted about seeing her
And she liked it

The Difference Between Nerds And Geeks

I found William Gibson's Performa 5200CD
Hidden in a computer lab at a school
I don't know which novels he wrote on it,
But it was his first to have in internet connection

To get there, you had to jump from the bus
At a stop where it didn't stop anymore,
Tumble down a grass hill and sneak in
The computer lab through the backdoor

I walked in on him explaining
The difference between nerds and geeks
To Jack Womack

"Nerds love Star Wars;
Geeks love Star Trek," said Gibson
"It's that simple, Jack."

The Last Time I Saw Naked Raygun

The last time I saw Naked Raygun
Was on January 6th, 2017.
I headed toward the Concord early, but
I stopped by Madison Public House for a grilled cheese.

I had stopped drinking beer,
And I'd been drinking ciders.
After a couple of pints of a habanero-mango,
I didn't want the grilled cheese anymore.

Naked Raygun was playing a memorial show for Sean McKeough,
Riot Fest co-founder and owner of the Cobra Lounge.
Before I walked on down Milwaukee Ave,
The bartender and I did a shot in his honor.

At the Concord, there was an auction of signed treasures
From bands like Sleater-Kinney, NOFX, Descendants, Rancid,
And of course, Naked Raygun,
Among many others.

While browsing the auction items,
I ran into Pierre Kezdy.
I shook his hand and headed up to the show room.
I don't remember much after that.

I ran into a friend from Logan Arcade,
She and her friends invited me to do a shot.
I remember that, and I remember getting
Another cider for myself.

I remember getting into an argument with some guy.
I remember slapping a beer out of his hand,
And him mopping it up with my coat.
I also remember that I was still wearing the coat.

I remember smelling of stale beer
On the train the next morning,
While my head invented new ways to ache
All the way to campus.

Precision And Collision

On tour in April of 1994
Self-proclaimed Precision and Collision
The Econoline belonged to Rodan
The Grifters had the Flower Shoppe van

At the Velvet Elvis in Pioneer Square
I went looking for The Grifters
"That should be easy," said Jeff Meuller
"They're the oldest ones here"

"What can you not hear with those in?"
Dave Shouse asked about my earplugs
"Pain," I said
"Good answer," he agreed

After the last Seattle show
At a club then called The Moe
I slow danced with Tara Jane O'Neal
To a Nancy Sinatra song

Missed Connection

In early March 2006
Flying from Alabama to California
To interview for a job at *Ride BMX*
In Houston, I missed my connection

I was on standby all day
I saw Paul Wall at a gate
His brown eyes met my blue
And I said, "What it do?"

A head nod and a peace sign
Followed by a quick grill flash
Then he stepped first class
Onto a flight to Las Vegas

Paul Reubens

On April 12, 2004, I drove to L.A.
For Peter Lunenfeld's 42nd birthday
Geert Lovink was in town
Dark Fiber, Uncanny Networks, Nettime

Coco Conn and I stepped outside
Benjamin Bratton was on the porch
I'd met him at her house the last time
When I saw Mark Pauline by the back door

The next day Douglas Rushkoff was in town
Doing a reading in the Hollywood Hills
Coco and I drove there with a friend of her daughter's
For years after that, Doug thought she and I were a thing

Before the talk, out the giant window
In Julie Hermelin's living room
I saw Paul Reubens
Rolling his garbage cans to the curb

Episodes in Erewhon

The Depths Of Dawn

A multitude of seeds
Waiting to spawn on the lawn
A blazing ball of heat,
Blistering the morning sky
Like a disease parting the trees,
Soon the party line will be all one sees

Greeting the day
With fleeting grey
Clouds float by
In a fake midday sky
A bird contemplates the air
Perhaps to fly

Our shadows stretched out
Like the road before us
Through fogging lenses,
We saw countless squirrels and birds,
Three rabbits, and one lone deer,
All meeting the morning with disparate goals

Under the covers of blue,
A half moon peeks in on the morning
A faint spiderweb foregrounds corn crops
And scenery fumigated by fog
The pine stands stoic as the sun rises behind it
Pointing straight up from the depths of dawn

Various Chirps

Both curious and cautious,
Cows are as apprehensive
As they are attentive

In the evenings,
A croaking chorus of frogs
Sings to the cotton-candy sky

Evening rain,
Like hope for boats,
Leaves a heavy haze on the morning

The midday sun
Burns right through this canopy of leaves
The only semblance of shelter along the route

All the chattering of humans
Wending through the wires
Can't reach the whispers of clouds in blue

A spider hung her hammock
In view of a field of fog
Overlooking a rumor, you can't prove true

Acres of it
Lying low like a giant reclining ghost
Disturbed only by birds of various chirps

Outcast Outpost

A tree cradles the dawn
Limbs aflame
Folds of molds
Halted fossils
A morning of two minds
Resurfacing

Shapes and shadows
Wires and whispers
Wind-whipped weeds
Glimpses of ourselves
In muddy bubbles

An avian eclipse
In alien flora
An outcast outpost
Under overcast clouds
A picture
No caption can capture

Thankfully Few Cars

Most noticeable in the back-wood backroads at dawn
is the sound: silence broken only by the chirps of birds and bugs.

There are thankfully few cars,
those roaring, rolling creatures of capital.

Their traces are all around though:
Roads, tire marks, oil spots, signs.

The sun eases up overhead,
scorching dirt, asphalt, and skin alike.

Like a god and a demon all in one,
The oppressive source of all life out here.

Animal Math

Birds hide secret messages
In the structure of their nests
Messages woven in twigs and plastic
Their brains synchronize
When they sing duets

Chick-a-dee-dee-dee-dee
Chickadees sound different alarms
Depending on the size and threat
Of approaching predators
The more *dees*, the more danger

The sky is a landscape
Of invisible wind gusts
Currents rising and flowing air streams
An Andean condor can coast
For over a hundred miles

Bees make maps
Denoting landmarks in dance
Bacteria vote
With signaling molecules
Mice count ants

When humans see something cute
A specific part of our brain gets excited
When an elephant sees us
The same part of their brain
Lights up

Strays

The Perfect Metaphor

Daily hanging in my head heavy.
And no matter what, I never feel ready.
Always slightly flushed, like you just came,
The flesh of your cheeks recalls hips of the same
Like the perfect metaphor that brings meaning to light.
The irony being that their meaning invites night.
It invites actions not illuminated, hidden by lacks thereof.
Lust, it seems, is a lot like love.

The desire lines in my head all lead to the same thought:
Paths less traveled but worn with want.
Lines of longing lingering on soft curves and in soft sighs.
Crossing in colored flecks, undefinable in your eyes.
Meeting in places impossible to touch.
Coming together in the middle, all of it all at once.
Absolute bliss or a close approximation thereof.
Lust, it seems, is a lot like love.

[January 30, 2011]

Body Language

Your soft moves in every word
And the million subtleties of your smile
An undiscovered science of silence
A linguistics of movements and gestures

Then the foreign language of that dress
And its silent dialog with your curves
An unknown tongue flowing over you
In fragments and run-on sentences

I try to understand, but I'm stuck on the surface
Tracing the hems of your dress with heavy eyes
Thoughts of you slowly sliding out of either end
Or of slowly sliding underneath

Your language of grace betrays my best effort
To remain innocent, quiet, and disengaged
I am a plaything for whatever your eyes say
And a slave to any hint beyond them

[December 19, 2010]

A Prayer For A New Year

More stretch, less tense.
More field, less fence.
More bliss, less worry.
More *thank you*, less *sorry*.

More nice, less mean.
More page, less screen.
More reading, less clicking.
More healing, less picking.

More writing, less typing.
More liking, less hyping.
More honey, less hive.
More pedal, less drive.

More wind, less window.
More in action, less in-tow.
More *yess*, less *maybes*.
More orgasms, less babies.

More hair, less cuts.
More ands, less buts.
More map, less menu.
More home, less venue.

More art, less work.
More heart, less hurt.
More meaning, less words.
More individuals, less herds.

More verbs, less nouns.
More funny, less clowns.
More dessert, less diet.
More noise, less quiet.

More courage, less fear.
More day, less year.
More next, less last.
More now, less past.

[December 31, 2007]

This Time

What we want from this time
is to see beyond the sublime
to more than live, but to feel alive
and never cease to strive
to be more than a metaphor
for all the people who came before
to leave marks and traces
evident on our peers' faces
to know upon leaving one day
that we've proven there's another way
to be, to do, and to thrive
to more than live, but to feel alive.

[January 31, 2003]

Lunch Hour

I fight hard not to swallow the moment whole
Struggle to spread the taste out long and thin
And to enjoy the slender morsels
To let them linger with the few and the far-between
The chasm of clock ticks and calendar pages
The aching hunger of days in-between
The latent longing stirred to life
With tears that swell from the gut and into the eyes
More of a revelation than an accident
To purposefully stumble into knowing bliss
Smiling with my eyes closed
My core alive with the soft gurgle of monarch wings

[December 23, 1998]

Coffee Cup

The long-awaited move
From a rut to a groove
Another session of passive aggression
Made the transition all too smooth

My decision had long been made
Far too long had I stayed
All of my frustration lost in the translation
Only a husk of the role I'd played

As she charged me, I didn't look up
Hands clutched around my half-empty coffee cup
Feeling more affection in the swirling convection
I did my best not to interrupt

I don't know what it means
So I'll take it for what it seems
Looked deep in her eyes and realized
She'd given up on all of my dreams

[March 6, 1998]

A New Day

This day is sickness
This day is disease
Tomorrow needs quickness
Tomorrow needs ease

Get on with the future
Get on with the mending
Finish up the suture
I want my happy ending

Today I no longer need
I'm writhing for tomorrow
This voice I'll no longer heed
These lips yield only sorrow

I lie in wait of a new day
That silhouette on the horizon
The eclipse of hope and dismay
When next the sun is rising

[May 21, 1990]

Acknowledgements

◆

First up, I have to thank the Close To The Bone crew, the most supportive group of derelict wordsmiths I've ever been a member of. Those folks have kept me going and kept me writing through several kinds of chaos. The First Cut is the deepest! Thank you all.

To Stephen J. Golds for taking a chance on me. I've been writing poetry since I could write, but it was never taken as seriously as it was by him. And to Craig Douglas for making it all happen. It's truly an honor to have them put this out.

To Josh Edwards, Gary J. Shipley, Peter Relic, Scott Wozniak, and Rebecca Cantor for kind and encouraging words.

To Lily Brewer for everything. As always... I can never say.

To all the people and places in these poems. Even the bad ones.

And to the people who published some of these before:

- *San Diego* and *Baldwin Park, Savannah* were in Sledgehammer: http://www.sledgehammerlit.com
- *Pale Blue Eyes* and *In Chicago* previously appeared in *Anti-Heroin Chic*: http://heroinchic.weebly.com
- *Tell Me Twice* also appears in the Pure Slush anthology, *Conversations* (2021).

I drew the Sharpie doodle on the cover in homage to *Honorary Astronaut* by Nate Pritts (Ghost Road Press, 2008), the book that brought me back to poetry. Thank you, Nate.

And thank you for reading.

[All poems written 2020-2021, except where otherwise noted.]

Printed in Great Britain
by Amazon